GIMP for Beginners

First 12 Skills

Gabriel Kuhlman

This book is dedicated to my rich dad.

Better than a poor dad.

-G

This work is copyrighted material.
©KuhlmanPublishing

For permissions or to use the same images we are using, please find us at our Facebook page at:
https://www.facebook.com/WritePublish/

ISBN 978-1-7943-1912-1

Introduction

Thank you for purchasing this book.

GIMP for Beginnners - First 12 Skills was created for people just like you who want to learn how to get the most out of GIMP. So, with you in mind, we created this step-by-step tutorial guidebook detailing the first 12 skills new users need. Learning any new software program is never an easy process. We hope this book will help you as you continue learning this new powerful software program.

The best way to learn a new program is to have a competent teacher who'll teach you all the steps necessary to complete this or that task. To help you learn as you go, we have provided all of the images we will be using in this book of tutorials for you on our Facebook page (address found on Copyright's page). These images are license-free images we found on Pixelbay, Pexels, and other license-free image websites.

Find these images under the category - **Learn GIMP**. Of course, if you'd prefer to use your own images, that is perfectly good. We just want you to have fun and learn.

Table of Contents

Other Books by KuhlmanPublishing

<u>Books by Frank Walters</u>

The Affinity Photo Beginner's Guide - First 10 Skills

The Affinity Bible - Part I

The Affinity Bible - Part II

Learn Affinity Photo
Top 10 Artistic Techniques

Learn Affinity Photo
Top 10 Most Popular Techniques

Learn Affinity Photo
Top 10 Portrait Techniques

<u>Fictional Titles:</u>
The Rooted Ocean Series - Submerged, Immersed, Engulfed (Author: Charlotte Birch)

The Drakkoyyn Series - Emergent Fire (Author: Aldane Walker)

The Girl Who Woke the Dragons (Author: John Zakour)

Other Photo-Editing Tutorial Books

The GIMP Bible
A Step-by-step Guidebook - Perfect for Beginners

Learn GIMP
Top 10 Artistic Techniques
Click here for this book

Learn GIMP
Top 10 Professional Techniques

Learn GIMP
Top 10 New Techniques
Click here for this book

How to Use This Book

This book is a step-by-step tutorial book on how to use GIMP 2.10. The techniques you will learn will give you a base from where to launch your skills.

Every tutorial has been created using high quality images and easy-to-follow steps that will help you on your journey from lost beginner to experienced user.

Please be aware that we have not filled this book with extra editorial information. This book is strictly a tutorial book on how to do different techniques. We purposefully limited our text to include only the information you need to perform each technique(s).

So, where we say to add this or that specific information, you should know that you are totally free to add any data you want to experiment with and to make your learning more immersive.

Once you understand the concepts of each technique and feel you have a firm grip on its application, then we hope we will have opened the doors of understanding (this program) wide open for you. Learning, we feel, is best done 'on the job'.

Save-As-You-Go
We highly suggest you periodically save your progress as you proceed through a specific technique. That way, if you make a mistake too big to correct, you can then re-open the image you are working on at the point when you saved it. Personally, this is a huge time saver for our editors. We practice this skill on every image we work with.

Using Our Photos
If you are going to use the photos we uploaded to our Facebook page, then we highly recommend that you download all of the images onto your desktop and place them in a single folder. That way, as you progress through this tutorial book, you can find each image we use in a very easy and stress-free manner.

1. Setting Up Gimp

Having a good understanding of the tools you'll be using in Gimp is the most fundamental skill you should learn.

In this first lesson, we'll not be going too deep. Why? Because all you really need is the basics when you are new to Gimp. It is in the working with your different images and making them more beautiful when you will learn how to use the different tools as effectively as you can.

We'll be covering some of the deeper functions of the tools in chapters 3-11 and in further books where we'll address different techniques and strategies to great editing.

i.   The basic layout of Gimp

The first thing you should do after you have downloaded Gimp to your computer is to click on the menu item "Windows" at the top of the UI and choose "Single Window Mode".

Here is a screenshot of how to do this:

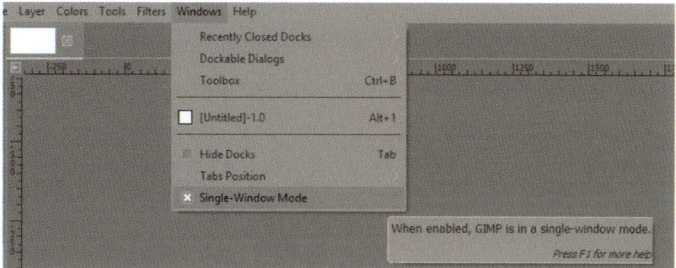

Once you have done this, you might see the UI in the middle of the screen with toolbars on either side of the main campus, like this:

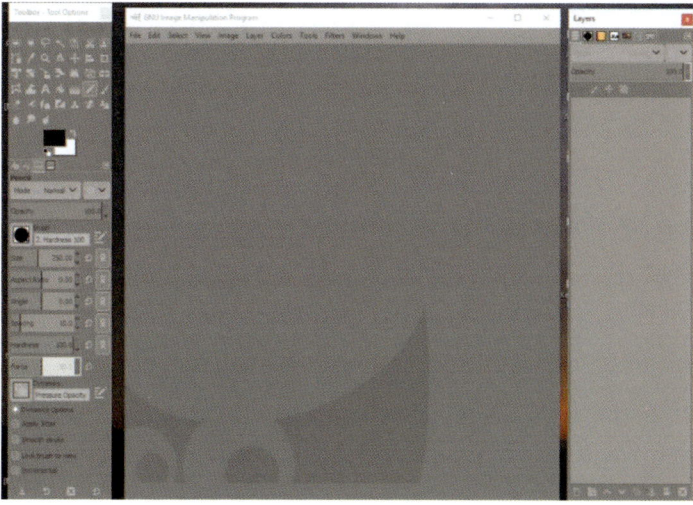

One trick to make your life easier while using Gimp is to set these toolbars (right & left sides) up so that they will be your default toolbars (i.e. they will always pop-up when you open Gimp).

To set these as defaults, click on **GIMP** and choose **Preferences**.

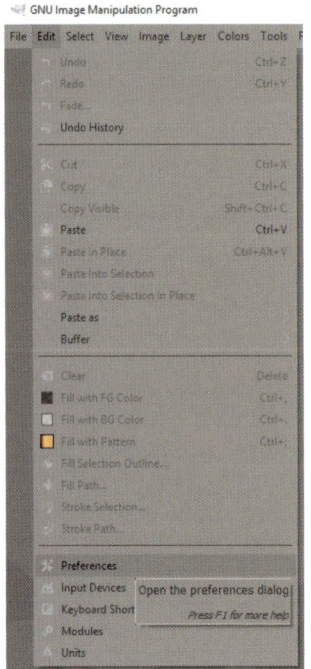

When you choose Preferences, a pop-up window will appear where you need to click on **Windows Management**. When you open this up, make sure the box is checked next to the "Save windows positions on exit" line (see orange square). Normally, this is already checked. If you are using an older version of Gimp, just make sure this is checked.

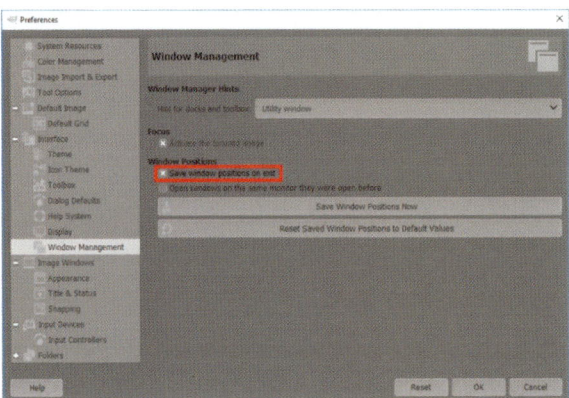

Next step is to click on **Tool Options** and click on the box next to *Save tool options on exit* and then press **OK**.

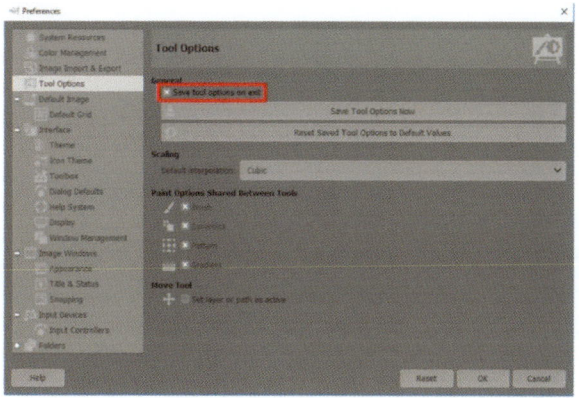

Now, whenever you open GIMP on your computer, every time it will open, you'll see it exactly how it is now.

Like most software programs, you will now need to reboot GIMP in order for the changes to take effect. Simply **Quit** GIMP and reload it to your desktop.

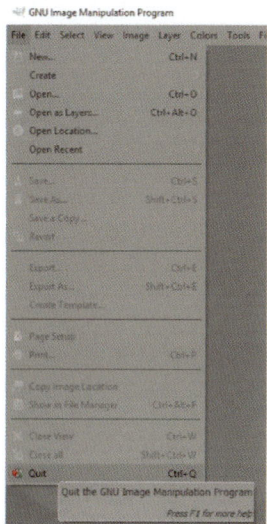

When it's reloaded, it should look something like this:

With this opened, let's take a look at the different parts of the User Interface (UI).

Some of you may already have some toolboxes on the left and right sides of the main canvas, but if you don't follow along. If you do, read what we have here for this step and see if there's anything here that can help you.

To set up GIMP the way we want it to look each time we upload it, let's do this:

1. Click on Windows and choose **Toolbox**.
   This will create the vertically-stacked list of tool icons (see in image above – far left).

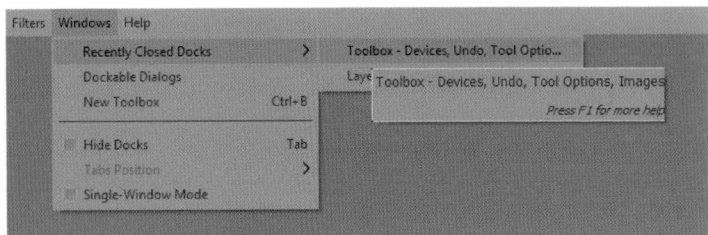

2. To compress this toolbar from a vertically-stacked list to more of a box, move your mouse to the circled UI icon (three parallel lines) and click & drag the pointer to the right.

When you drag these parallelly-stack bars to the right, the Toolbox will shrink like this (in the top left side of the UI:

We want to move these **Tool Options** below the **Toolbox**. To do this, click on the words "Tool Options" and drag this whole box to the left side of the UI and under the Tool Box. Once you have dragged the **Tool Options** under the **Toolbox**, the **Tool Options** window will now be located under the **Toolbox**.

Actually, doing it is much simpler than explaining. Play around with this and you'll figure it out in no time.

2. How to Open Images

In this tutorial we will show you a couple different ways of <u>how to open images</u> onto the Gimp canvas.

Ready?

Ok, let's here are the steps:

1. *Click* **File**.
2. *Click* on **Open**.
3. *Click* on **Search**.

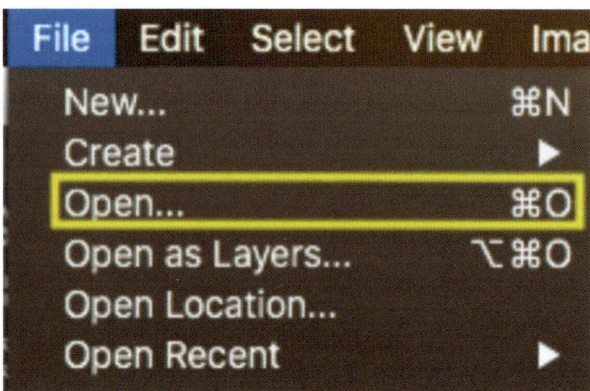

Here you can search by *typing* a name and then *hitting* enter.

4. *Click* on **Recently Used.**

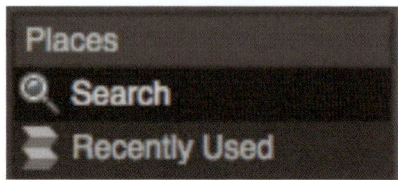

Here you can *choose* one of the recently opened images.

When you *click* on one of them, you will see a preview.

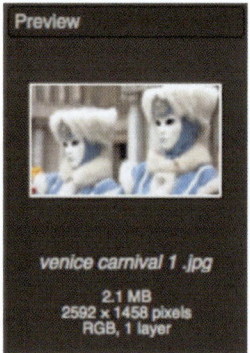

In this list we can search in our computer for our image folder. This can be time consuming, but I will show you a way how we can do this much quicker, the next time we want to go to our image folder. When we have found the folder, don't open it yet but only *select it*.

By *clicking* on the little cross here below left and *click* it, we can *add* the folder to this list which makes it quicker to access the next time we need it.

Now *double click* on the image folder and *select* the image you want to open.

5. Look at the preview and hit **Enter**.

6. *Go* to **File**.

7. *Click* on **Open**.

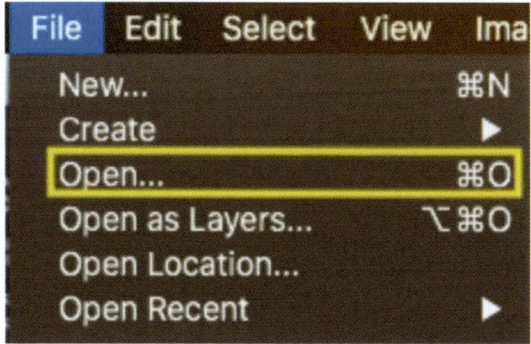

You can select multiple images by *holding down* **Shift** and then *selecting* the other images you want.

When we *click* **Open** or *hit* **Enter** they will all open as separate images and we can *edit* them separately.

8. *Close* all images by going to **File** and **Close All.**

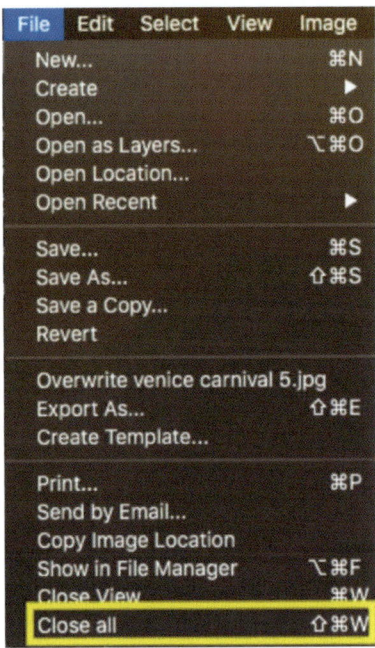

9. *Go* to **File.**

10. *Click* on **Open as Layers.**

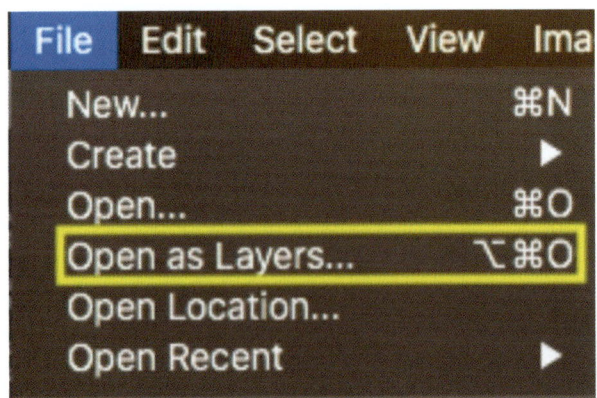

11. *Double click* on the image you want to open it.

12. *Go* back to **File.**

13. *Select* **Open as Layer.**

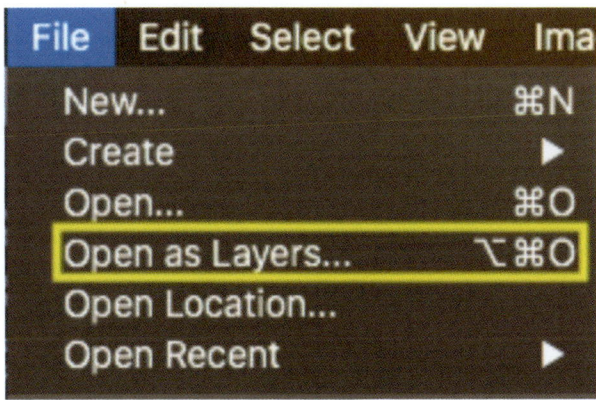

14. *Double click* a second time.

This will open as a new layer on top of the image that you've already opened, and not as a new image.

Go back to **File** and **Open as Layers** and select while *holding down* **Shift**.

Several images open and you will see that they all open as layers in the same image.

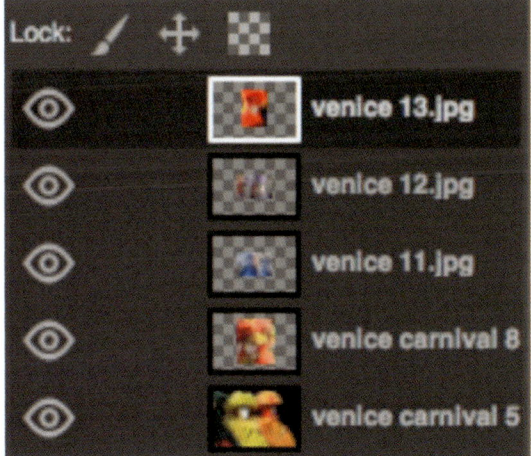

Go to **File** and **Close All** and then **Discard Changes.**

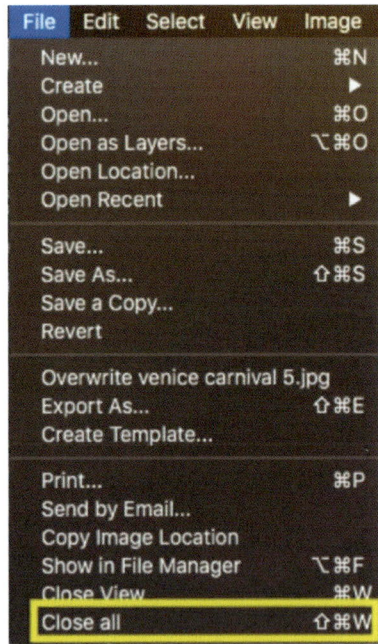

Go to **File.** We can also *click* on **Open Recent** to open an image, when we do this again the next image will open as a new image.

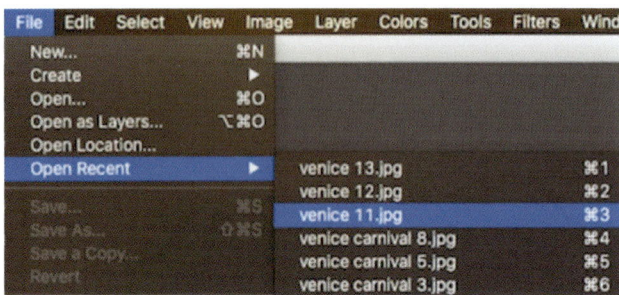

Ok, we will now close all and look at yet another way of opening images. Go to **File**, *click* **Close all** and *click* **Discard Changes**.

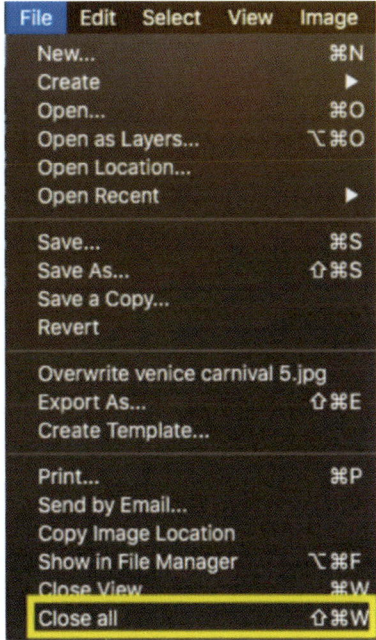

Close Gimp *go* to your image folder, *right click* the image you want to open and *select* **Open With,** then *click* on **Gimp**.

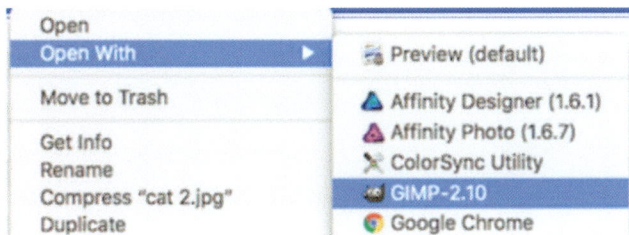

If Gimp is not open yet, it will open.

When we open another image this way, it will open as a new image.

We will *close* both these images by *clicking* on **File** and **Close all**.

Still, another way to open an image is to use **drag & drop**. When we do this again with a second image, it will open as a new layer. When we now *select* multiple images, and *open* them by **drag & drop,** they will all *open* as layers.

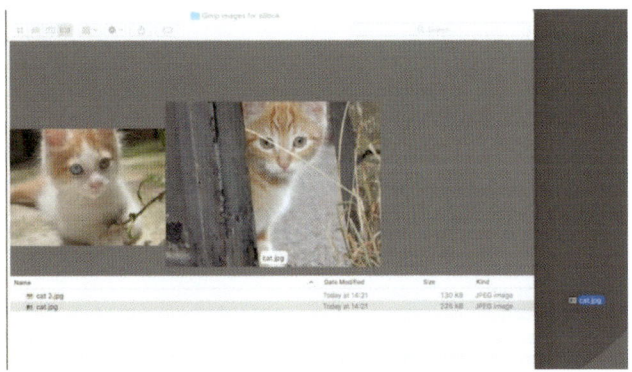

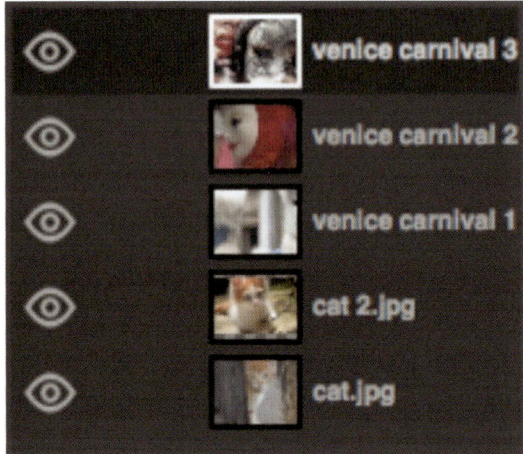

Go to **File** and **Close All** and then on **Discard Changes**.

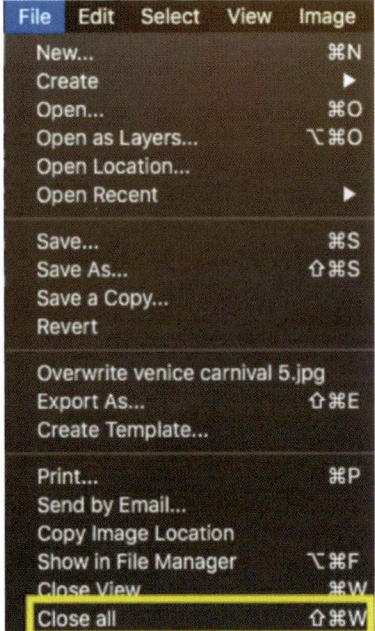

Select again multiple images and *open* them by **drag and drop.** Because there is nothing opened yet, now they will all open as a new images and not as layers.

You now know different techniques to opening images in Gimp.

3. What are Layer Masks and How to Use Them

In this tutorial, we will show you <u>what layer masks are and how to use them</u>.

If you want to use the same image we'll be using, please download the image from our Facebook page.

Ready?

Ok, let's begin...

A Layer Mask is like a see-through film you place over a layer used on photo-manipulation software like GIMP, Affinity Photo, and Adobe Photoshop.

Masks are a fundamental tool and knowing what they are and how to use them will be integral to all your photo-editing skills.

To understand how to use Layer Masks, you'll need to download the two images we will be using in this tutorial - the girl and a rainbow-colored image.

We suggest you save them onto your Desktop. This is the easiest. Once you have the two images, click on **File** and **Open as Layers**.

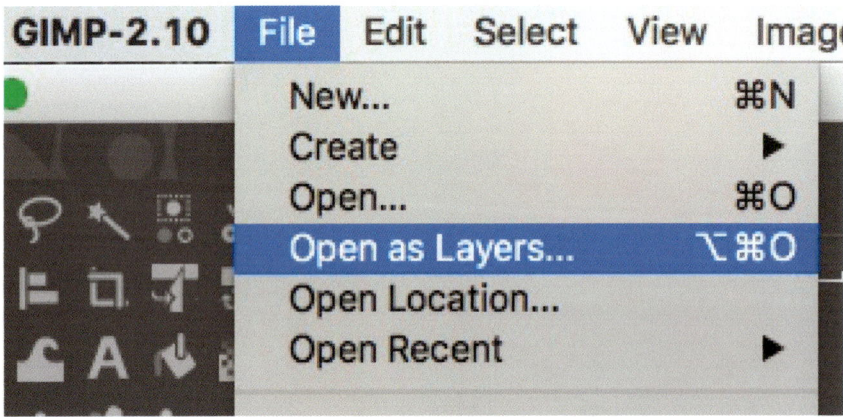

Once the images have been loaded onto GIMP, they should look like the image below. There are two layers - a <u>base layer</u> (bottom of the stack) and the <u>active layer</u> (see white border around the Rainbow layer).

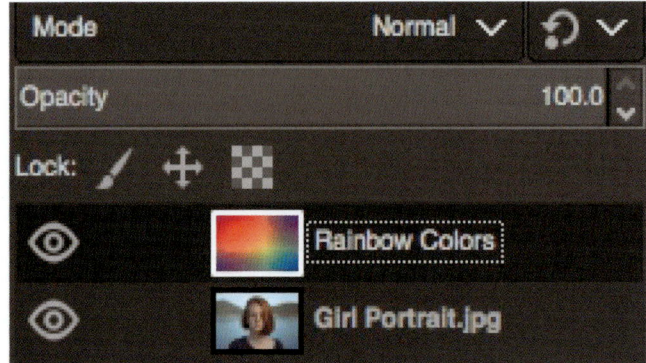

Let's now right-click on the layer you want to add the **mask** to (i.e. the *Rainbow Colors*) and the **Context Menu** will pop-up and here you should choose **Add Layer Mask**.

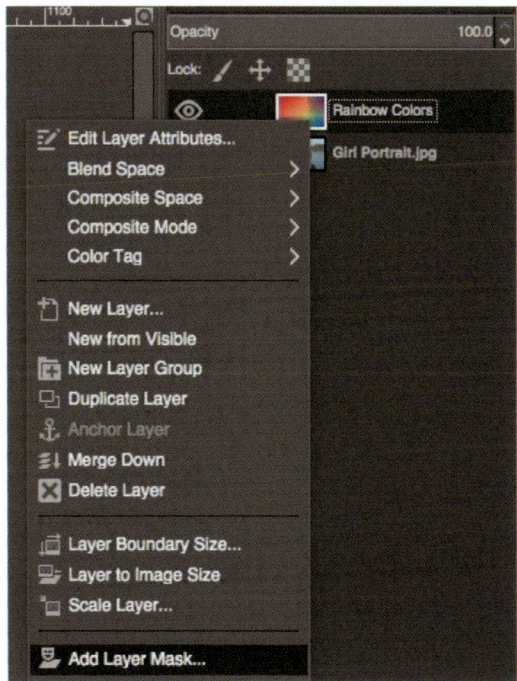

This will bring up the Add Layer Mask pop-up window (image here).

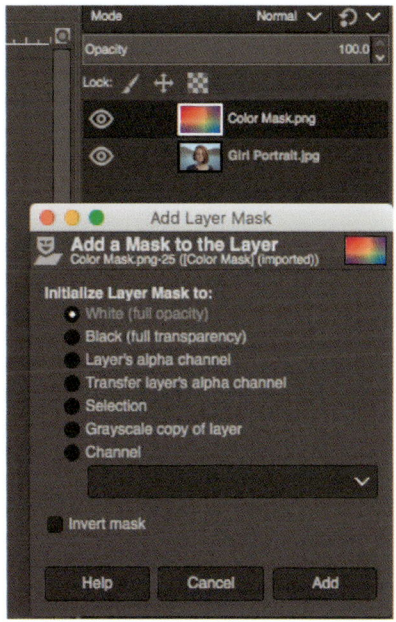

What are **Layer Masks**?

Layer masks allow us to see a layer as either 100% <u>visible</u> or 100% <u>transparent</u>.
These **masks** compromise three colors (**white**, **black** and **gray**) and control the transparency of a layer.

White means 100% visible.
- Full opacity
- No transparency from the mask

Black means 100% transparent.

For the sake of this tutorial, let's select a **White** (full opacity) mask and press **Add**.

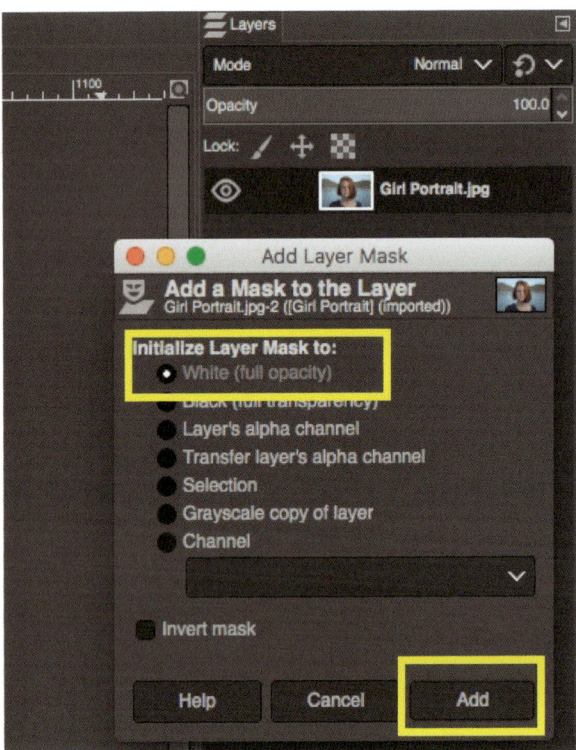

Immediately after pressing **Add**, there will appear a **white box** on the Rainbow Color layer.

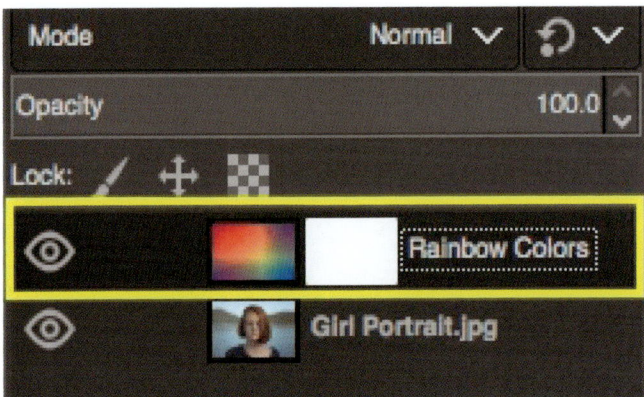

The layer mask has now been added to the Rainbow Colors layer. It is also active (there is a white border around the thumbnail in the dialogue, but is not visible due to the mask being white as well) and ready for modification.

At this point any operations performed on the canvas will apply to the mask and not to any layers themselves. To illustrate how masks can affect its layers transparency, let's paint!

I am going to use the **Rectangle Select Tool** to select roughly the top third of the image, and I'll fill this selection with black.

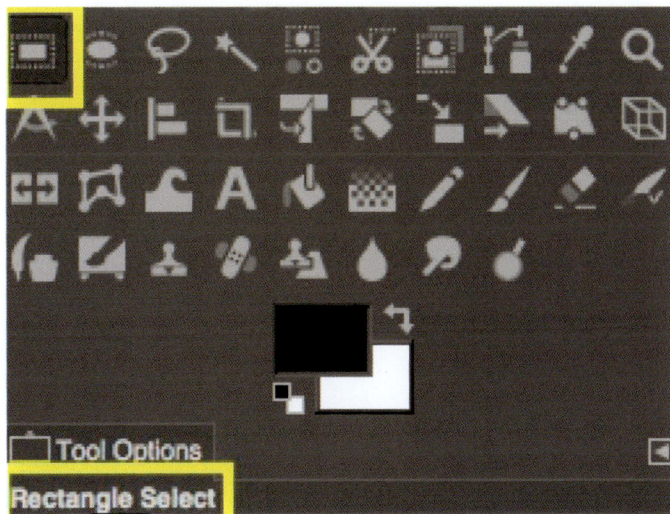

Using the **Rectangle Select Tool**, let's select the top portion of the image.

You can see the selected portion of the Rainbow Colors layer.

I want to fill this selection with black, but before I do I need to make sure that my foreground color is black. Click on the foreground color in the **Color area** to bring up the "Change Foreground Color" window.

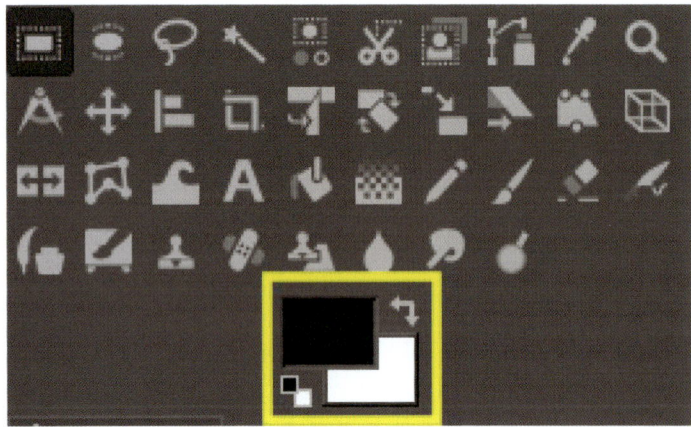

Click the foreground color to change.

The **Change Foreground Color** window allows you to set the foreground color. For this tutorial, make sure all the values are 0.0. This will make the color black.

Note: In this case, the foreground color was already black. But, in the future event it is not, now you know how to change the foreground color to black :).

With the foreground color set, you can now use the **Bucket Fill Tool** to fill in the selection.

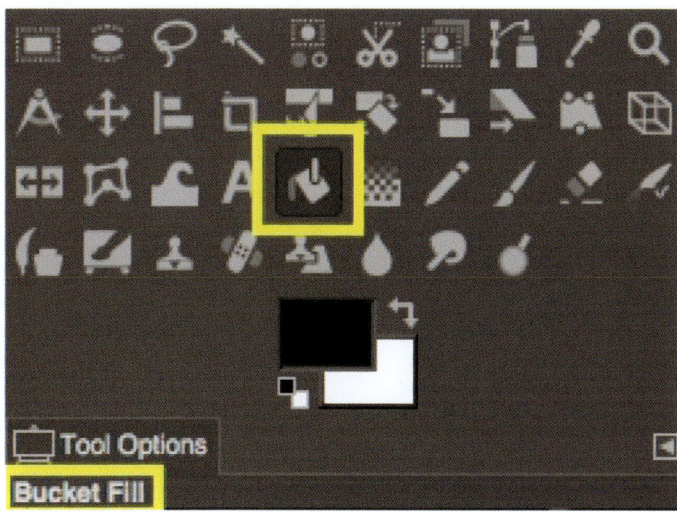

Once you click on the selected rectangle, you will immediately see what's beneath the Mask. Painting in Black makes the underlying layer visible.

Remember from above?   **White** means 100% visible.   **Black** means 100% transparent.

 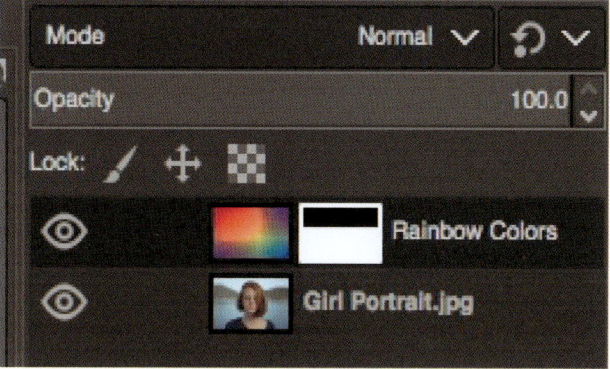

As you can see, filling the selected portion of the layer mask with black resulted in that area having 100% transparency, showing the layer below it.

If you do a **Rectangle Select** operation on a different area of the mask, you can fill it in with a different shade of gray to produce a variable opacity. For example, I will select a few different regions of the mask, and fill it with different levels of gray:

 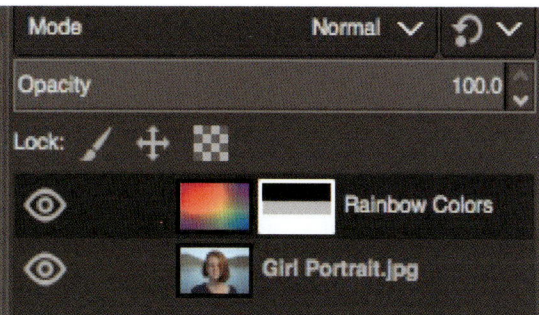

If you examine the layer mask, you'll see that there are different levels of gray being applied (black to white, from top to bottom), and their value is what determines the opacity of the layer.

<u>Selective Colorization Example</u>

A good example of the application of layer masks is doing selective colorization of an image (selectively allowing color to show through a mostly black and white image). I'll walk through how to easily do this with an image of a football match.

Football Girls

Start the process by <u>duplicating</u> the base image by using the shortcut - **Shift+Ctrl+D.**

You can also simply click in the Menu Bar - **Layer** and then **Duplicate Layer**.

Then **desaturate** the upper layer...

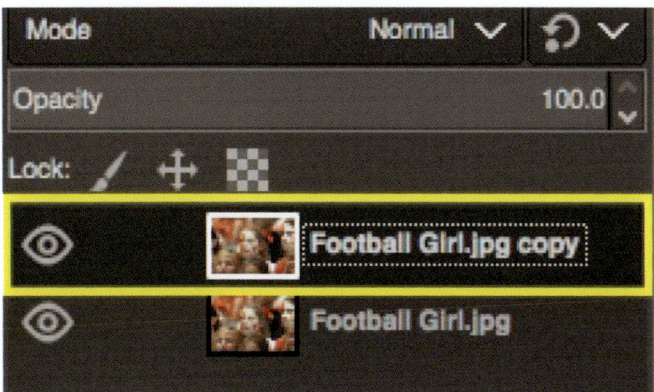

by clicking in the Menu Bar: **Colors** / **Desaturate** / **Desaturate**

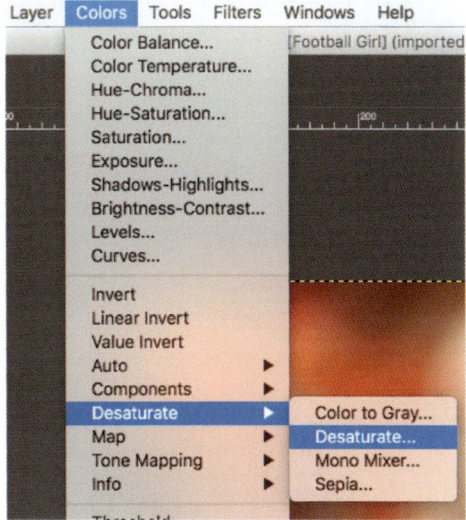

Now that the layer is desaturated (i.e. Grayscale), we are going to follow the same steps we did in the first part of this tutorial and right click on this layer and choose **Add Layer Mask**.

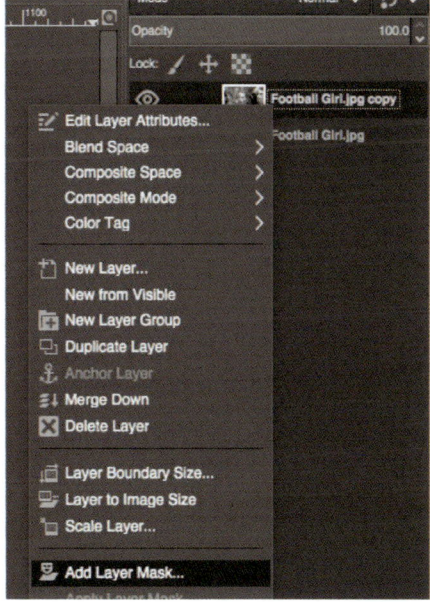

Because we want to reveal the base layer underneath the desaturated layer, we want to make sure we choose **White** (full opacity).

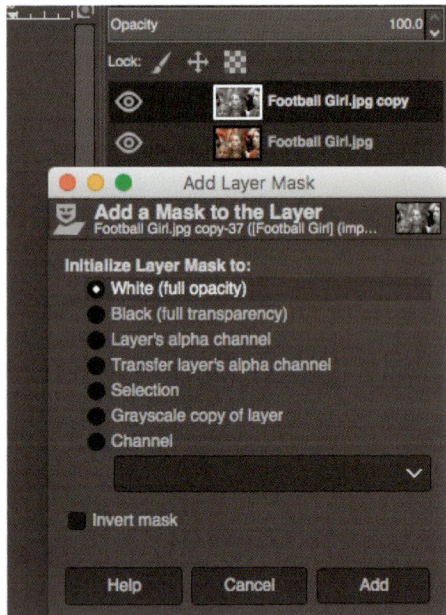

At this point, the Layers window should look like this:

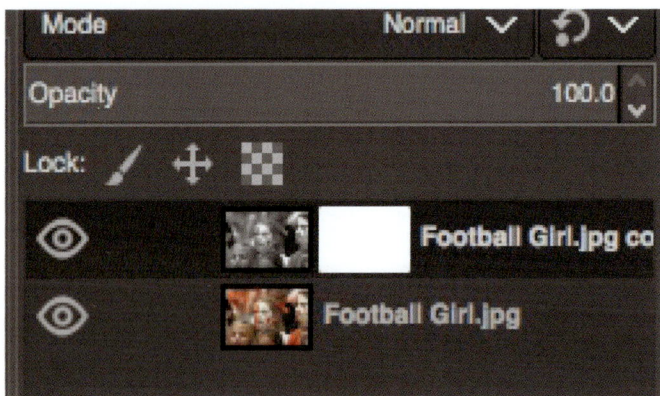

As before, set your foreground color to black.

This time, rather than filling selections, we are going to use the **Paintbrush Tool** to paint areas of the image we want the color to show through from the layer below.

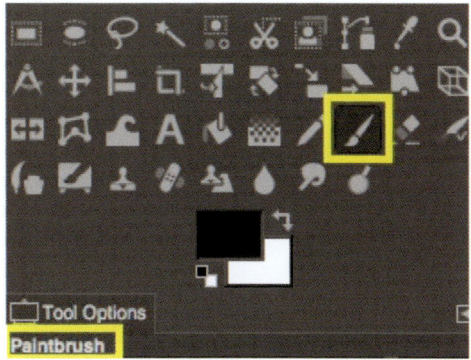

We are going to paint over the face of the girl in the middle. This will allow the colors to shine through the mask. The rest of the image will keep its desaturated (Grayscale) appearance.

And there you have it. A basic, but hopefully a very clear explanation of what Masks are and how to use them.

4. How to Crop an Image

In this tutorial, we'll learn a couply ways of how to crop images.

If you want to use the same image we'll be using, please download the image from our Facebook page.

Ready?

Ok, let's begin.

The first way of cropping an image:

1. *Click* on **File** and then on **Open.**

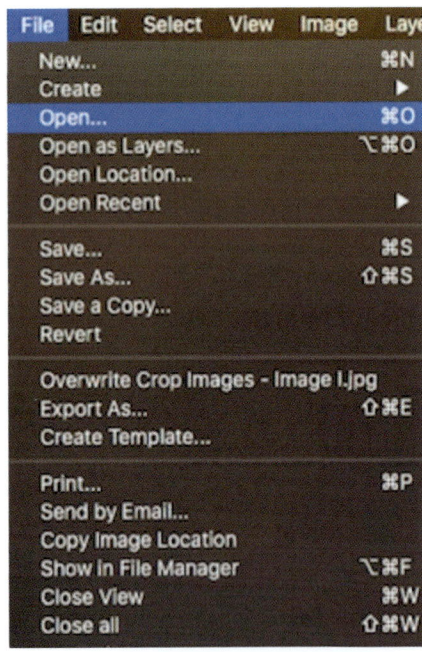

2. *Select* your image you want to crop (In the preview you can see, if you have the right image).

3. *Click* on **Open**.

4. *Click* on **View** and then on **Fit Image in Window.**

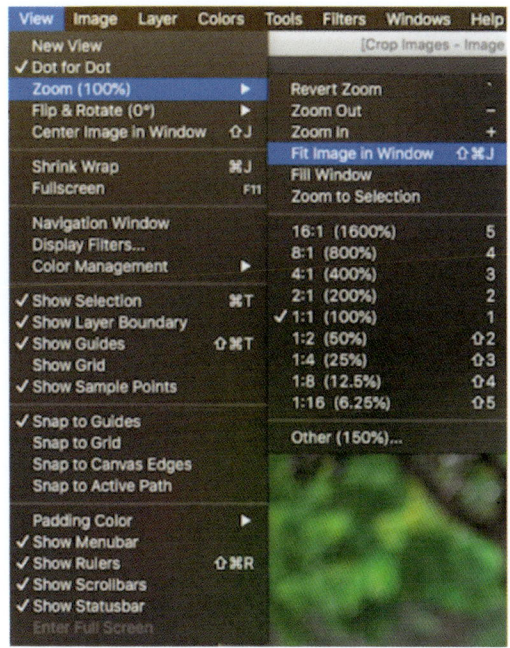

5. *Select* the **Crop Tool.**

6. *Click & drag* to make our cutout.

By *clicking* and *dragging*, the handles and or the corners, we can make corrections and when we *click & drag* inside the image, we can *move* the whole cutout.

7. *Press* **Enter** or *click* in one of the corners to **Apply**.

Another way of cropping an image is by using the **Rectangle Select Tool.**

1. Go to **Edit** and *click* on **Undo Crop Image**.

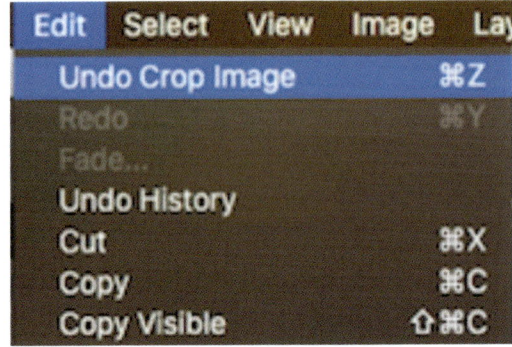

2. *Select* the **Rectangle Select Tool.**

3. *Click & drag* to make a selection.

Here too, we can, by *click & drag* the handles and or the corners, make corrections. When we *click & drag* inside the image, we can *move* the whole selection.

1. *Press* **Enter** or *click* in one of the corners to apply.

2. *Go* to the **Menu Bar**, *click* on **Image** and then *click* **Crop to Selection**.

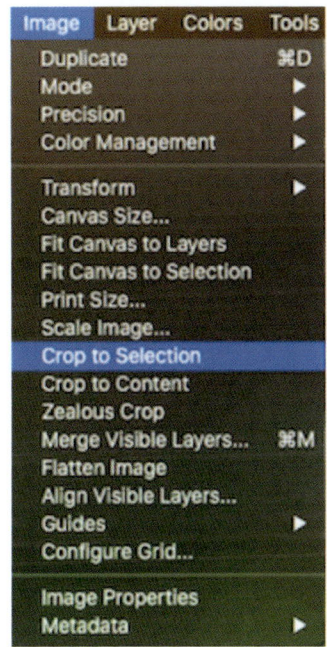

To save our work:

1. *Go* to **File**.

2. Click **Overwrite Crop Images**, so we overwrite our existing image.

3. Or we can *click* **Export As** and *export* the cropped image under a new name to whatever folder we like.

And this is the end result:

5. How to restore Lost Tool Options and Lost Layers Panel

Ever have the problem of disappearing Tools? For new users, this is a recurrent problem. Hopefully, this tutorial will solve many future frustrations for you.

When, for some reason, the tool options are removed from their default position, we can *place* them back by *going* to the **Tool Options** tab and then by *clicking & dragging* move it back to its original position.

When the **Tool Options** are completely gone, like this, we'll *go* to the **Menu Bar**, *click* **Windows**, **Dockable Dialogs** and then **Tool Options.**

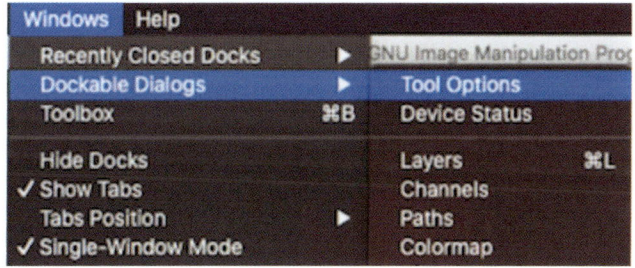

GIMP will place the window back, but on the right hand side.

By going to the **Tool Options** tab, we can *click & drag*, and move the window back to its default position.

We can do the same with the layers panel when it is not on its default position.
Grab it by the **Layers Tab** and *click & drag* it back to its proper position.

When it has disappeared all together, like this, we go to **Windows**, **Dockable Dialogs** and *click* the option **Layers**.

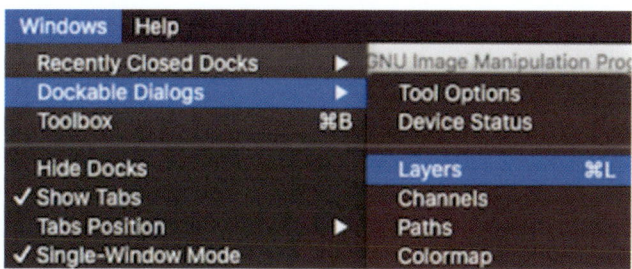

Gimp will place it back on the right-hand side. By *click* and *hold* on the tab we can *drag* it to the first position. *Click* on the tab so the layers become visible. In this way we can *change* and/or reposition it, all the **Dockable Dialogs** to our own preferences, or we can restore the default settings.

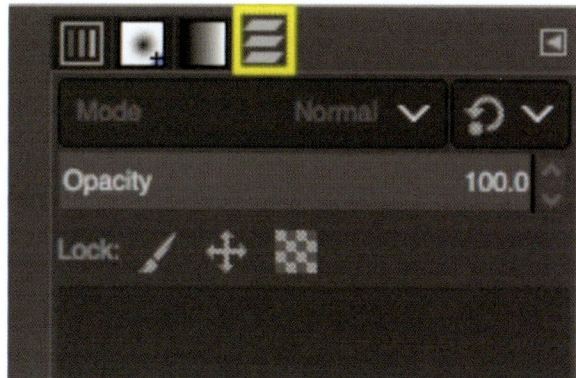

Restoring Gimp to its default settings can also be done in the following way:

I will first reposition two windows as an example.

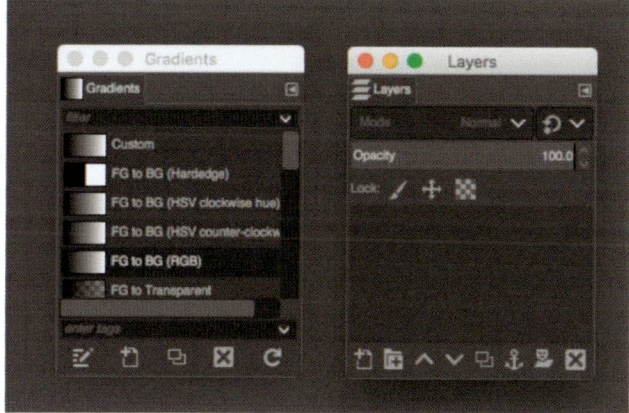

1. *Go* to **Gimp-2.10** in the menu bar.

2. *Click* on **Preferences.**

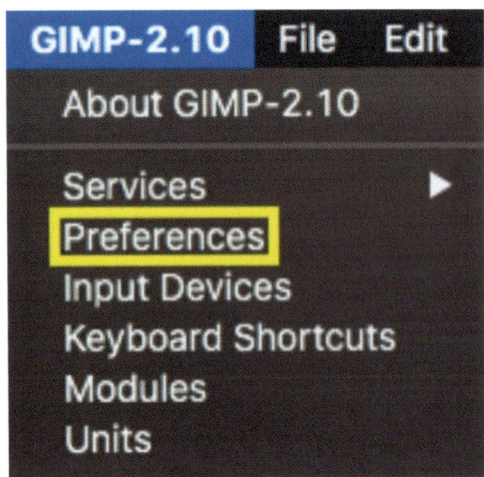

3. *Select* **Window Management.**

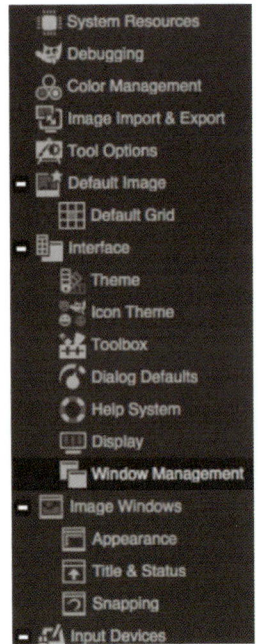

4. *Click* **Reset Saved Windows Positions to Default Values**.

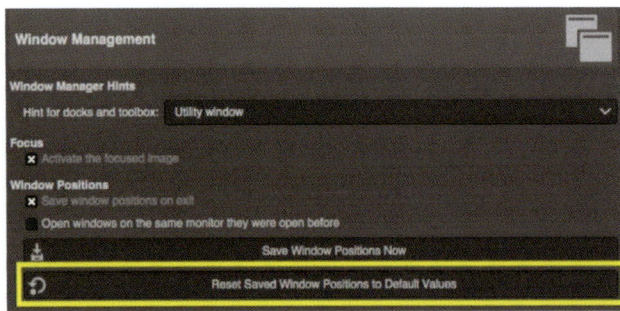

5. *Click* **OK** and then **Ok** again.

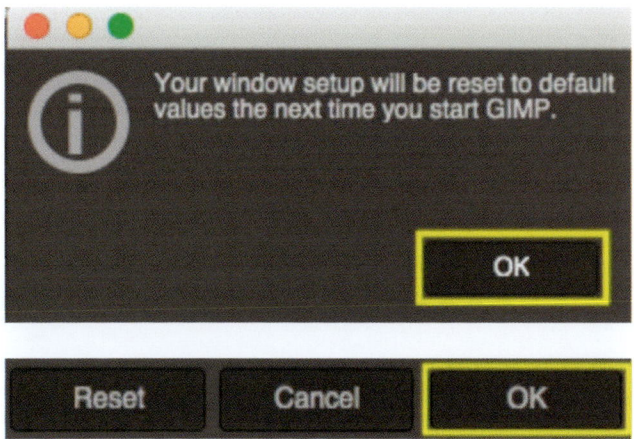

Now we *close* Gimp and when we reopen it, it opens in three separate windows.

Enlarge the main window if necessary and *click* **Windows**, and then **Single Window Mode.**

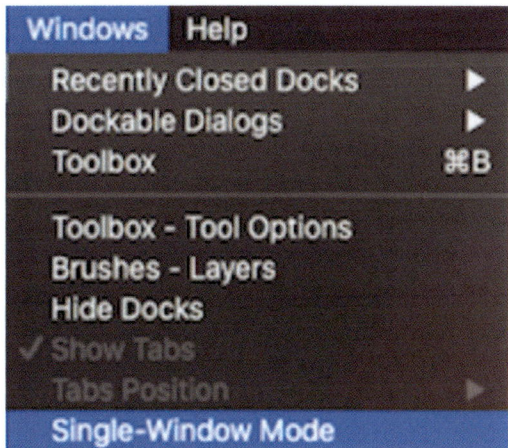

Maximize the window. *Click & drag* on the edge of the **Toolbox** to *enlarge* it a little.

When we *close* Gimp now it will reopen with these settings.

One last tip: When we accidentally hit the tab key, this will happen.

To undo this, we just need to hit the **Tab** key again. And that is it.

And that concludes this tutorial.

6. How to Use the Text Tool

In this tutorial, we'll learn how to add text to an image.

If you want to use the same image we'll be using, please download the image from our Facebook page.

Ready?

Ok, let's begin by opening the image we are going to use for this tutorial onto the GIMP canvas.

1. When we have opened our image, we click on the **Text Tool** in the **Toolbox**.

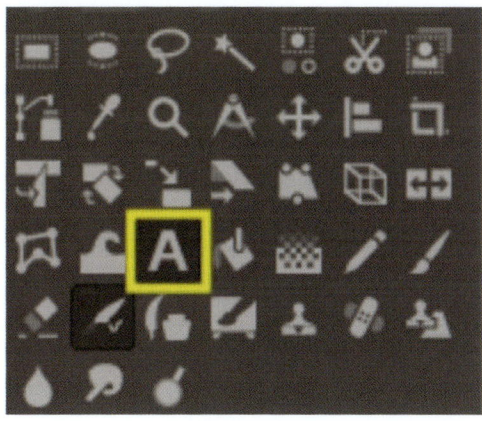

2. The tool options will open and we will we will start by enlarging the size, because otherwise the begin text will appear very small.

3. Type in **100**.

Later, we can always make our text larger or smaller.

4. Now click in the image where the text should start. There will appear a small work window above it.

5. Start typing the text. In the layer box will appear a text layer which is active.

6. Click enter to make a new line.

The size of the text area adjust itself automatically.

7. To choose another font, we place our cursor above the AA icon and turn, without clicking, the mouse wheel.

We can see that the font of out text changes. So, this is an easy and fast way to choose our font.

If we already know what font we want to use, we can fill in the first letters and the font name will show up.

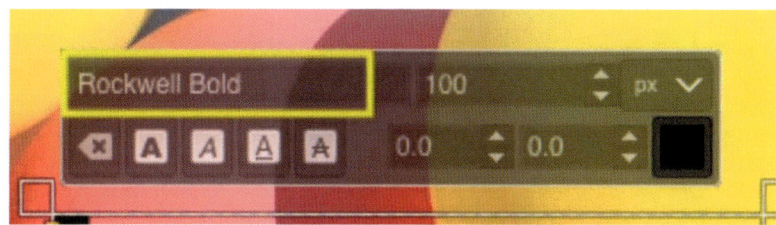

Now, let's make our text a little bit bigger.

Select the **text** by *clicking & dragging* the whole text to the right.

We can type in a certain value, but when we click on the little triangle (see image), the text enlarges with every click, so we can exactly see what we are doing.

Deselect the selection.

The words have now the proper size, but are partly outside the image.

To change this, let's *click* on the **Move Tool** in the **Toolbox**.

We must click exactly in one off the letter, so we can see the cursor changing in the **Move Tool**.

Then we can, by using *click & drag*, move the entire text to exactly where we want it.

Select the **Text Tool** again and select the whole text.

Let's now look at some further options of the Text **Tool**.

Here, we can change the text to bold, to *italic*, <u>underline</u> it or ~~strike it through~~.

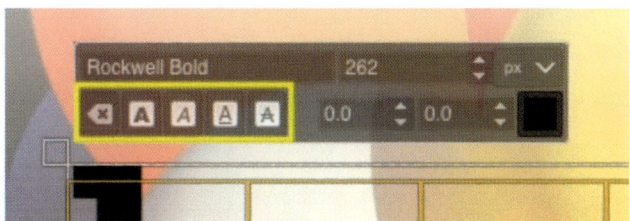

Now, *deselect* the text.

In the **Toolbox,** we can choose the options <u>left justified</u>, <u>right justified</u>, <u>centered</u> or <u>filled</u>.

Here, we can adjust the <u>line spacing</u> (up & down arrows) and the <u>spacing between the letters</u> (ab).

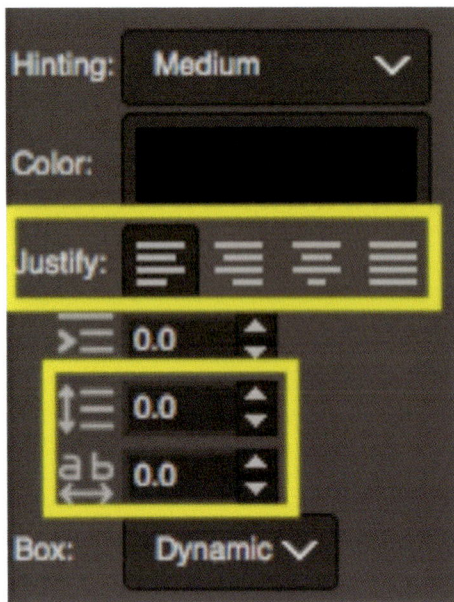

We are going to change the color of the first word.

Already, the **Text Tool** is selected and the text layer is active.

Double-click on the first word.

Go to the work window and click the **color** option (see black box circled in yellow).

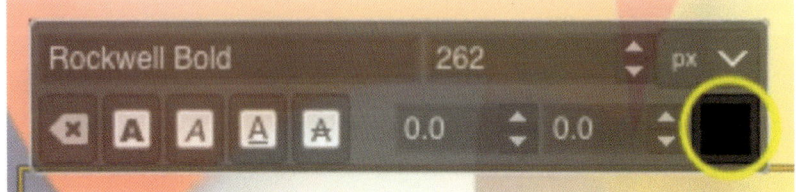

Here, we can choose our color, in this case **blue**.

Click **OK**.

Deselect the word.

Go to **Foreground-Background** option and click on the **white** color (or click on the double-arrows to change their positions).

Click & drag it to the second word.

This word becomes **white**.

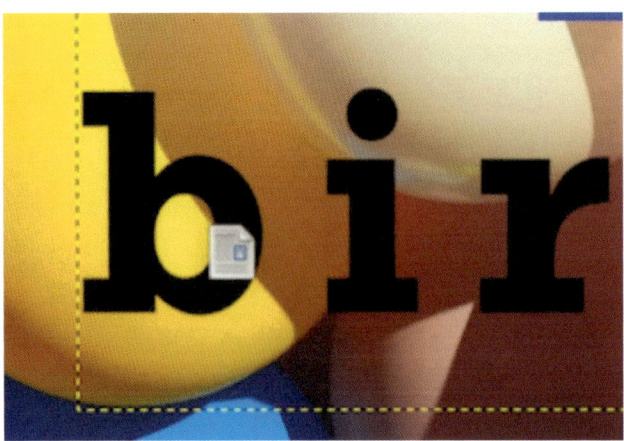

We can do this with any color that is selected in <u>foreground and background</u> option.

Click **Filters** in the **Menu Bar**, **Light and Shadow** and **Drop Shadow**.

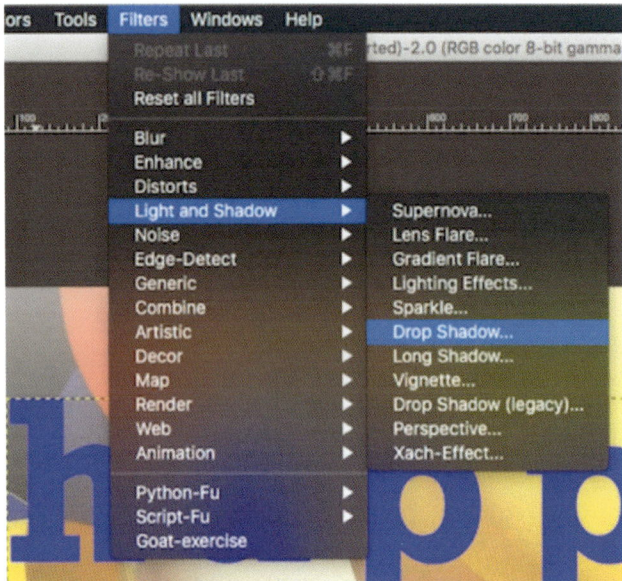

The values that we fill in here will be applied to the whole text.

We'll make the **X** and **Y** offset **10**.

This will give us a shadow right and below the text.

We can also fill in a negative value which will give a shadow on the left and above.

With the blur radius on the default **10**, we will get a soft-edged shadow.

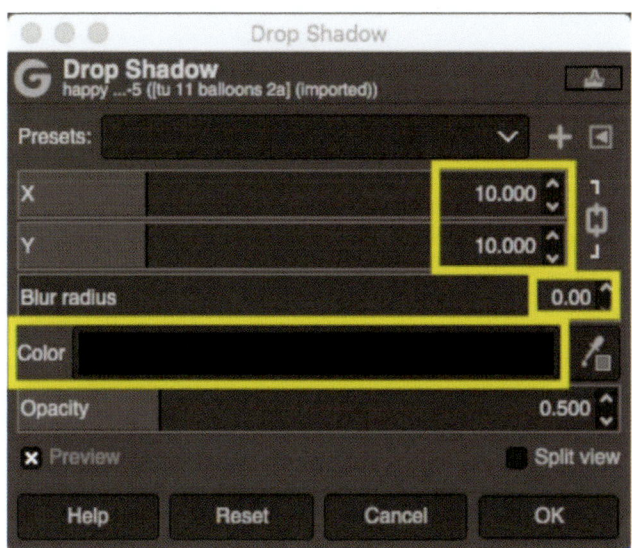

We will type in **0**, so we will get a hard edge.

Here we can choose the color of the shadow.

In this case, we'll choose **bright red**.

Change the **Opacity** to **2.0**

Click **OK** to see the result.

If necessary, we can undo our actions with **Ctrl+Z** (or make further adjustments by going back to the **Drop Shadow** option).

Now, let's select the **Perspective Tool** in the **Toolbox**.

Click in the image and drag to make a **Dynamic Perspective**.

Click **Transform**.

So, there we have it, the basics of the **Text Tool** with a little extra.

This is the end result:

7. How to Adjust Brightness & Contrast

In this tutorial, we will learn how to adjust Brightness & Contrast

If you want to use the same image we'll be using, please download the image from our Facebook page.

Ready?

When Gimp is already open, we can *open* our image folder, and bring the image that needs corrections into Gimp by **drag & drop**.

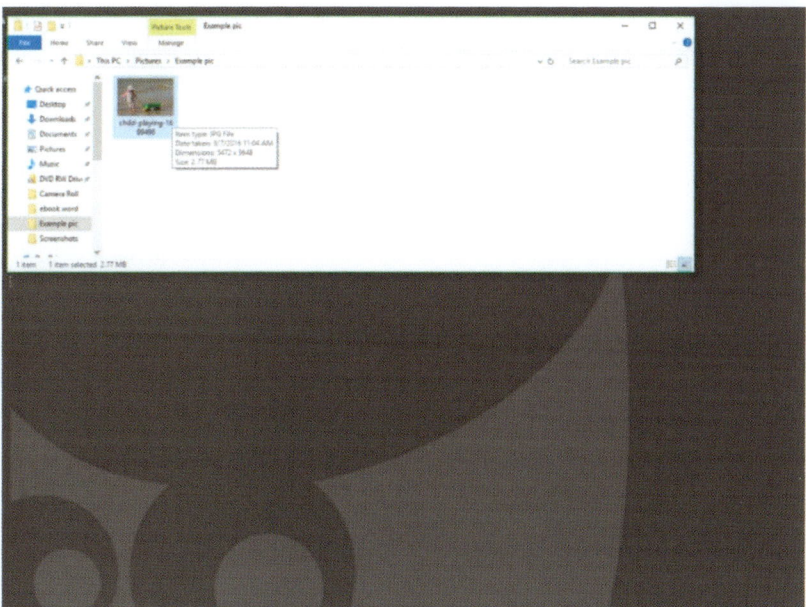

Then, we'll *click* on the **Zoom** icon in the top right-hand corner of the window to fit the image in the window.

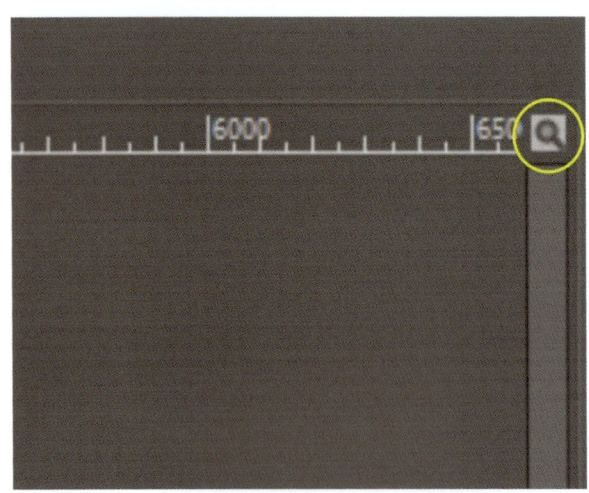

Go to the Menu bar and *click* on **Colors**.

Here, we'll *click* on **Brightness-Contrast**.

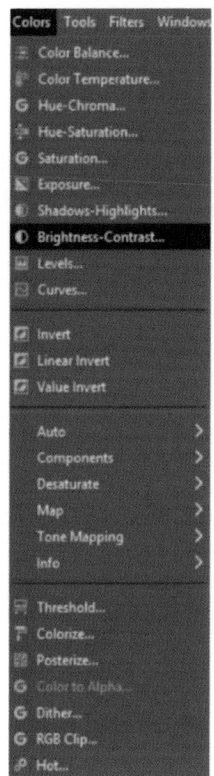

We can play around a bit with the sliders to get the desired result.

Click **Reset** to <u>start anew</u>.

For this image, let's make the **Brightness** <u>plus</u> **40** and the **Contrast** also <u>plus</u> **40** by <u>clicking 40 times</u> of both slider lines.

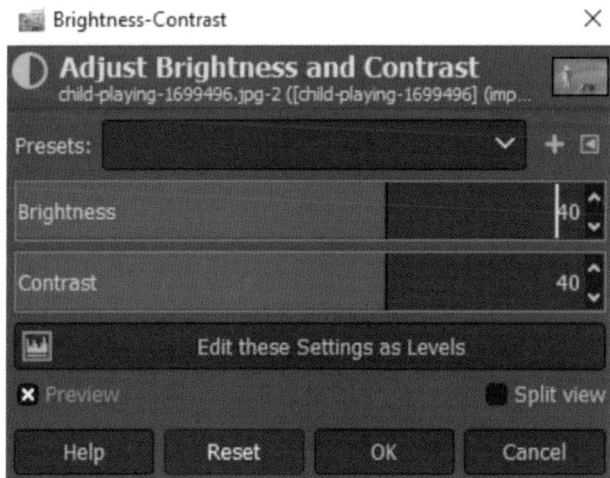

Click **Preview** off and on, to see the difference.

When we are satisfied with the result, we can *click* **OK**.

To save our work, go to **File**.

Here, we can overwrite our original image, or we can *export* it by clicking on **Export As**.

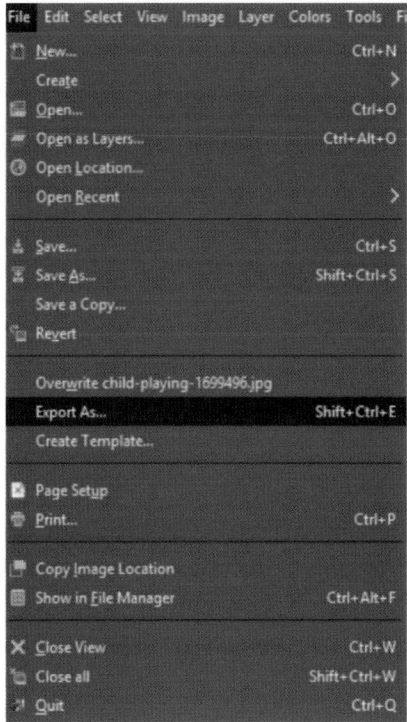

Now, we can give our image a new name. When done, simply press **Enter**.

GIMP-Image-How-to-adjust-Brightness-&-Contrast.jpg

When we *click* **Export**, we have saved our original as well as our new image.

And that is how we change the **Brightness** and **Contrast** of an image.

8. How to Use the Sharpen Filter

In this tutorial, we are going to learn how to use the sharpen filter.

If you want to use the same image we'll be using, please download the image from our Facebook page.

Ready?

Ok, let's begin...

Open your image folder and make a copy of the image you want to sharpen. We do this, so we can apply the sharpen effect on the copy. In this way we still have the original image, in case something goes wrong, or when the effect is not what we want after all.

1. Now *right click* on the thumbnail, *go* to **Open With** and *click* on **Gimp**.

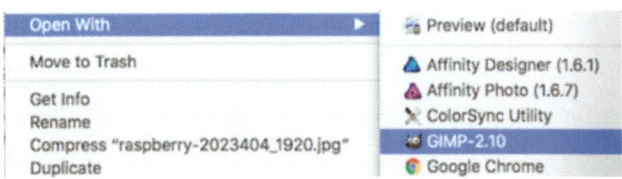

Usually it is better to sharpen an image at its final resolution, and, generally speaking, sharpening should be the final step in image editing.

2. When our image is open, we can, if needed, go to **View**, **Zoom** and *click* **Fit Image in Window.**

3. *Click* on the **Duplicate Button** at the bottom of the layers panel to *make* a duplicate.

We do this so we can compare the original and the sharpened image after we have applied the effect.

4. *Double click* on the name of the bottom layer and *rename* it **original.**

5. *Hit* **Enter**.

6. Then *double click* on the name of the top layer and *rename* this one **sharpened.**

7. *Hit* **Enter** again.

8. *Go* to **Filters**, **Enhance** and **Sharpen**.

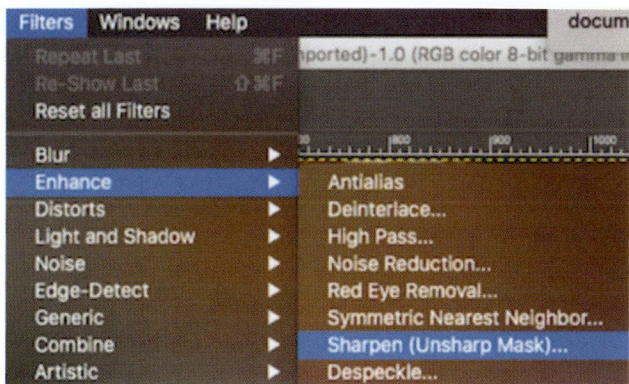

Gimp has renamed this filter from unsharp mask to sharpen. At presets, we can *use* a previous used setting. We can also *add* the current setting to the preset list, or manage the presets.

9. *Click* **Reset** to *go* back to the default settings.

10. With the radius slider we can *set* how many pixels on either side of an edge will be affected. High resolution images allow a higher radius.

11. For this image we *make* the **Value 4**. With the amount slider we can *set* the strength of the sharpening.

We should be careful not to *overdo* this. With most of the images, a subtle sharpening will suffice, unless of course we want to create a particular effect.

12. Here we *make* the amount **0.6**.

The threshold slider allows us to set the minimum difference in pixel values that indicates an edge where sharpening must be applied. So you can *protect* areas of smooth tonal transition from sharpening, and avoid creating blemishes in face, sky or water surface. For now we leave this as it is. We can *zoom in* and *or* out by *holding* down **Ctrl/Cmd** and *rolling* the mouse wheel. This can be done while the dialogue box is open.

13. *Click* the **Preview** *off* and *on*, to *see* the difference.

14. Or *enable* the **Split View**, which divides the image in before and after.

15. We can *click & drag* the split line.

16. When we *hold down* **Shift** and *click* on the line, we can *swap* the filtered and not filtered area.

17. And when we hold down **Ctrl/Cmd** and *click* on the line, we can *change* from vertical to horizontal and back.

18. When the effect is to our liking, we *click* **Ok**.

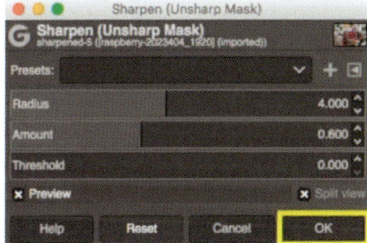

19. Now *click* the cye of the top layer *off* and *on* the *see* before and after.

And this is the end result:

Before:

After:

9. Path Tools for Beginners – Part 1 of 3

In this tutorial we're going to learn <u>the first technique on how to use the path tools.</u>

If you want to use the same image we'll be using, please download the image from our Facebook page.

Ready?

Ok, let's begin by opening the image we are going to use for this tutorial onto the GIMP canvas.

We start by making the **Paths Tool** active.
This can be done by going to **Tools** and then *click* on **Paths**.

Or we can just *click* on the **Paths Tool** icon in the **Toolbox**.

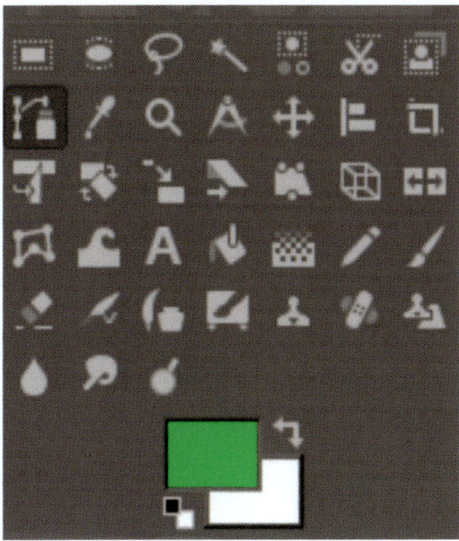

The shortcut for this tool is the **B** key.
The **Edit Mode "Design"** should be checked.

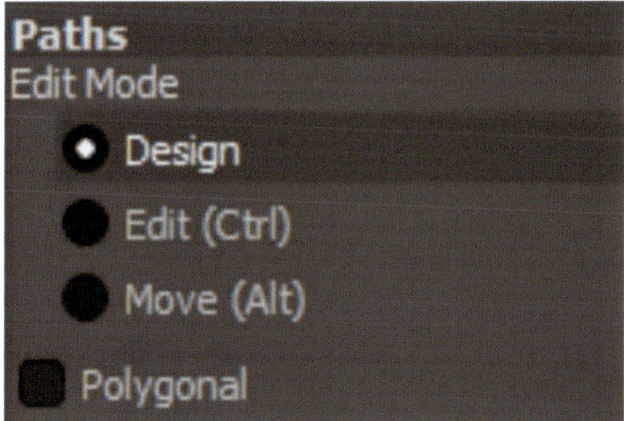

Zoom in to the object by holding down **Ctrl/Cmd** and *rolling* the mouse wheel away from you.

Click the first node. Then *click* the second node, but *hold* the mouse button down. *Drag* the handle out and *move* it to make a curve.

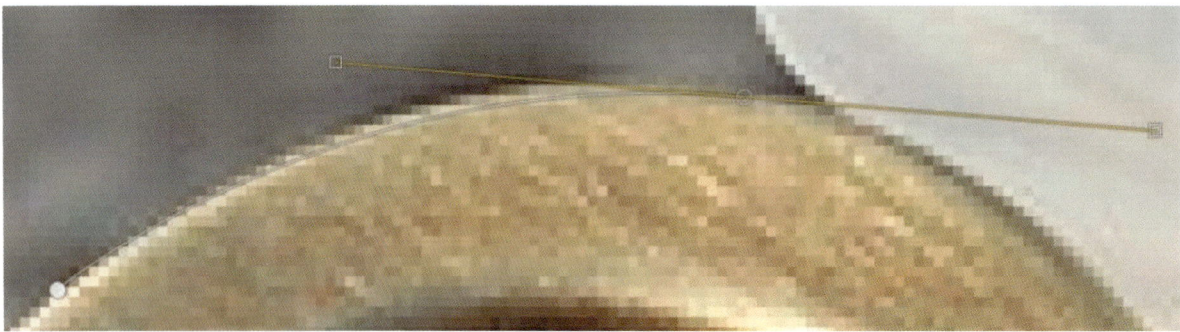

When the curve looks good, we can *let go* of the mouse button. Now *click & drag* the handle back to its node.

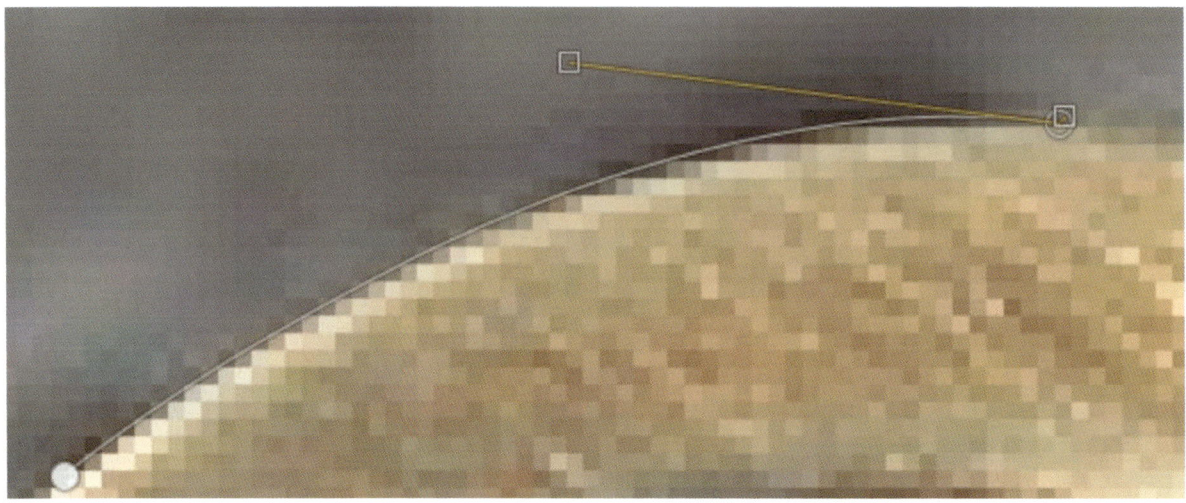

And then we can *click* the next node. And again, do *not release* the mouse button, but *drag* it out instead. Make a curve and then *let go* of the mouse.

Click & drag the handle back to its node.
Perfect. Now, we can make our Path, node after node.

When we *hold* the **Space bar** and *move* the mouse, we can *move* the image.

To make a straight line, just *click* a node and *let go* of the mouse.

We can *undo* with **Ctrl/Cmd+Z** and *redo* with **Ctrl/Cmd + Y**. Repeat this for the whole picture until you get to the first node.

When we are back at the first node, we hover with the mouse pointer over it. Then we *press* **Ctrl/Cmd** and when the chain icon is visible, we can *click* to close the **Path**.

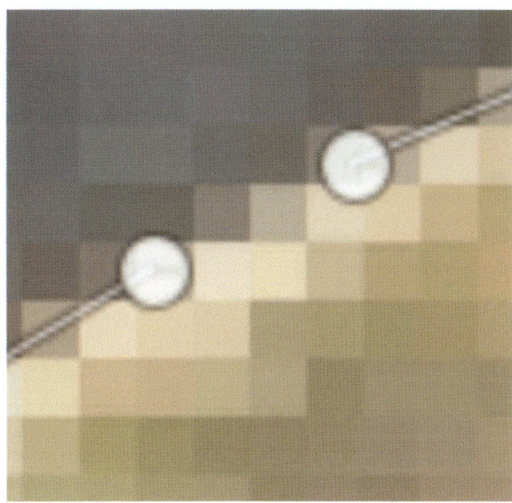

Now we can correct previous made nodes, by *clicking & dragging* them.

In this image we also want to *remove* this inner area. When the previous path is closed, we can start making a new Path by just *clicking* a node again. Then *click* the next one, *hold* the mouse button down and *drag out* the handle to make the curve.

Let go of the mouse and, by *click & drag*, move the handle back to its node. And we repeat the same process until we are back at the first node.

Then we'll hover over the first node, *hold* **Ctrl/Cmd**, and when we see the chain, we can *click* to close the Path.

Press **Ctrl/Cmd + Shift + J** to fit the image in the window. Now *click* the button **Selection from Path**, to change both paths into one Selection.

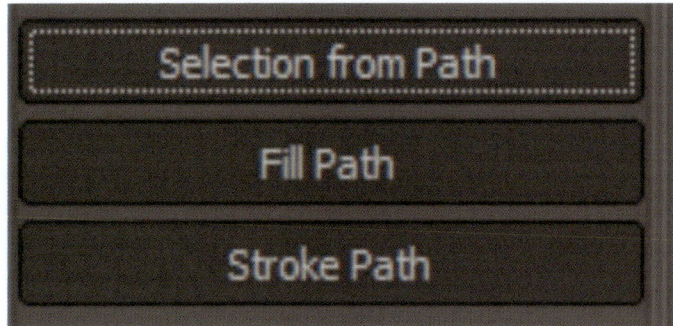

Then we can *click* **B** or *click* on any other tool to make the path invisible.

And that is how we can, in a simple and easy way, make very accurate Selections with the **Paths Tool**.

10. Path Tools for Beginners - Part 2 of 3

In this tutorial we're going to learn <u>the second technique on how to use the path tools.</u>

If you want to use the same image we'll be using, please download the image from our Facebook page.

Ready?

Ok, let's begin by opening the image we are going to use for this tutorial onto the GIMP canvas.

We start by making the **Paths Tool** active.
This can be done by going to **Tools** and then *click* on **Paths**.

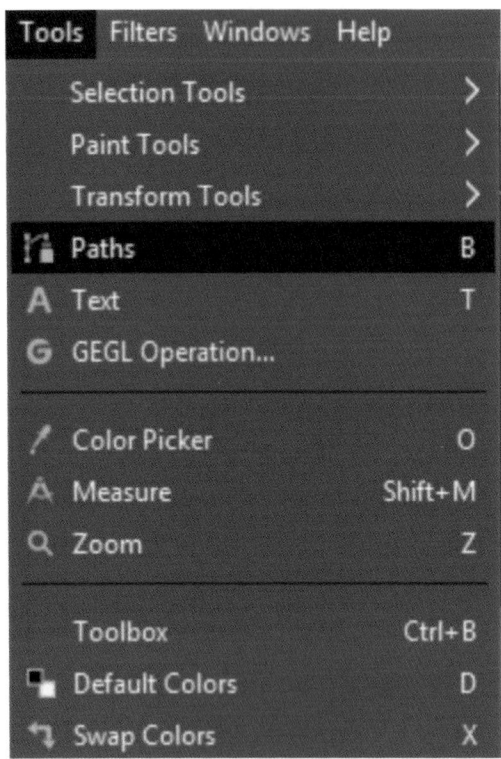

Or, we can just click on the **Paths** icon in the **Toolbox**.

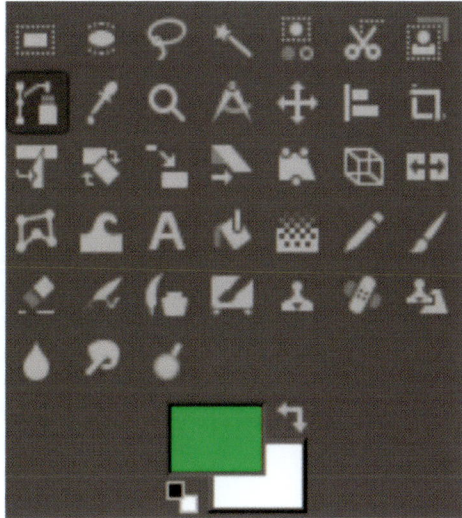

The shortcut for this tool is **B**.
The **Edit Mode "Design"** should be checked.

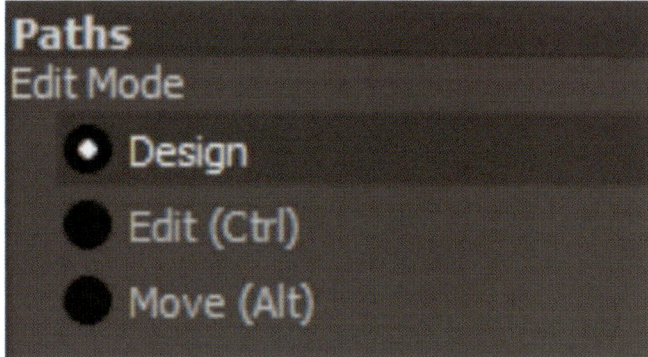

Zoom in to the object by holding down **Ctrl/Cmd** and rolling the mouse wheel away from you. Just *click* the first node or control point, then the next one and so on.

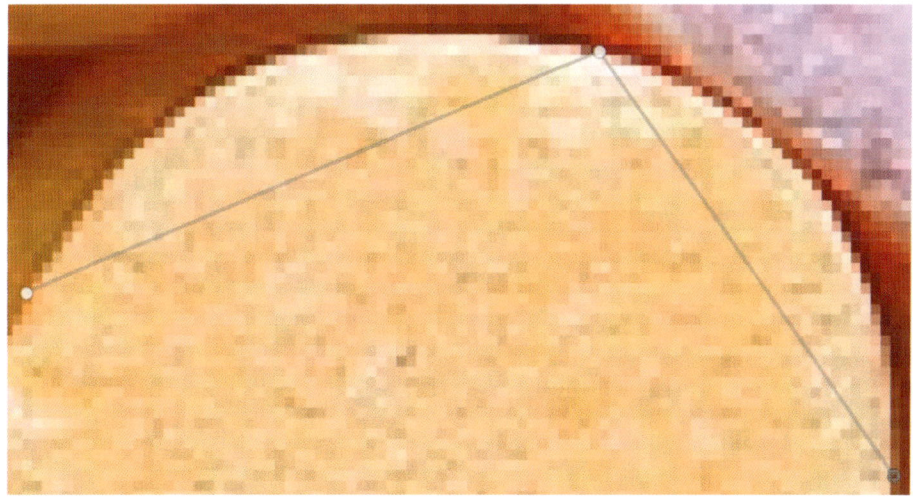

We will edit the straight lines later on.

Hold the **Space bar** down, and move the mouse, to move the image.
By pressing **Ctrl/Cmd + Z,** we can *undo* one or more previous steps, and with **Ctrl/Cmd + Y** we can *redo* them again. In this way we go around our subject.

When we are close to the first node, we hover the mouse pointer over it.

Press and hold **Ctrl/Cmd** and when the chain icon is visible, we can *click* to close the path.
By *clicking* and *dragging* a node we can still make corrections.

Zoom out or press **Ctrl/Cmd + Shift + J** to maximize the image in the window. Now we check the option **Edit**.

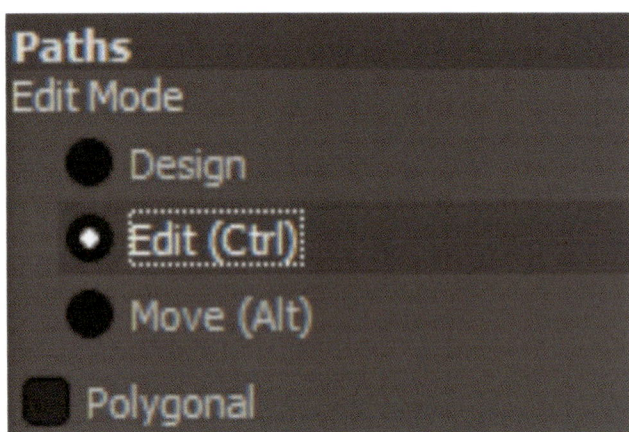

Zoom in again.

Click & drag a node on one of the lines, to make a curve.
When we *let go* of the mouse, we cannot move this node anymore, but we can *undo* it with **Ctrl/Cmd + Z**.

72

When the node is made, we can make corrections with the handles.

In this simple way, we can make our curves in the path.

When all this is to our liking, we can *click* on the button **Selection from Path**, to make the selection.

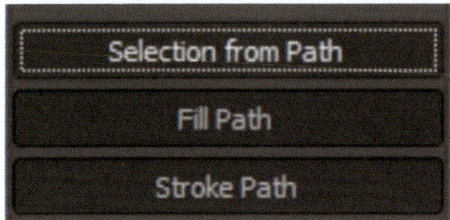

Then we *click* on a random tool in the **Toolbox**, to make the path invisible.

Or we *press* **B**.

This also makes the path invisible, but leaves the **Paths Tool** active.

And that is how we can, in a simple and easy way, make very accurate selections with the **Path Tool**.

11. Path Tools for Beginners - Part 3 of 3

In this tutorial we're going to learn <u>the third technique on how to use the path tools.</u>

If you want to use the same image we'll be using, please download the image from our Facebook page.

Ready?

Ok, let's begin by opening the image we are going to use for this tutorial onto the GIMP canvas.

We start by making the **Paths Tool** active.

This can be done by *right-clicking* in the image, going to **Tools** and then *click* on **Paths**.

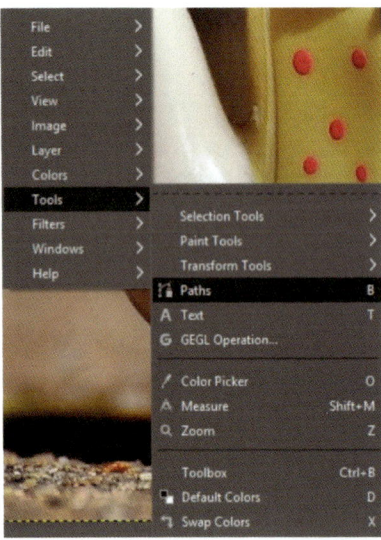

Or we can just *click* on the **Paths** icon in the **Toolbox**.

The shortcut for this tool is **B**.

The Edit Mode **Design** should be checked by default.

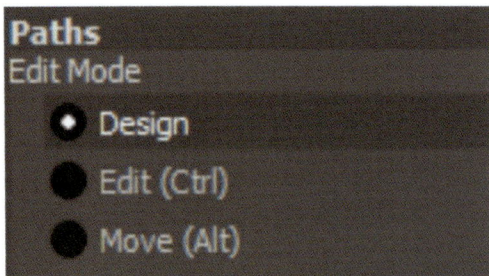

Zoom in to the object by *holding down* **Ctrl/Cmd** and rolling the mouse wheel away from you.

Click the first node. Then *click* the second node, *hold* down the left mouse button and drag out the handle just a little bit. Let go of this handle.

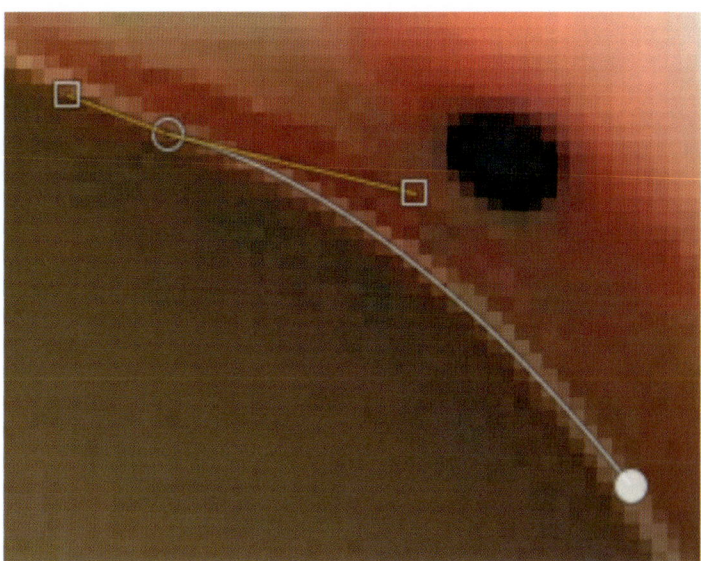

Now *click & drag* the other handle out, to make the curve.

When this looks good, we *click* the next node, *hold down* the left mouse button and again, we drag it out a little bit.

Click & drag the other handle to make the curve. In this way we can make a very precise selection with the **Paths Tool**.

When we *press* and *hold* the **Space bar** down, we can, by moving the mouse without *clicking*, move the image.
With **Ctrl/Cmd + Z** we can *undo* one or more previous steps, and with **Ctr/Cmd + Y** we can *redo* them again.
In this way we go around our subject. When we are close to the first node, we hover the mouse pointer over it.
Press and *hold down* **Ctrl/Cmd** and when the chain icon is visible, we can *click* to close the path.

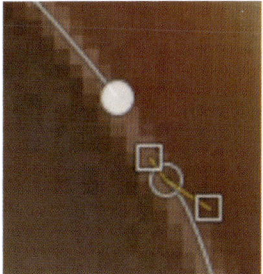

By *clicking* and *dragging* nodes we can still make corrections. Zoom out or press **Ctrl/Cmd + Shift + J** to maximize the image in the window.

Now we can, in the same way, make a second selection in the same image.

Click the first node. *Click* the second node, *hold* the left mouse button down and *drag* the handle out a little bit.

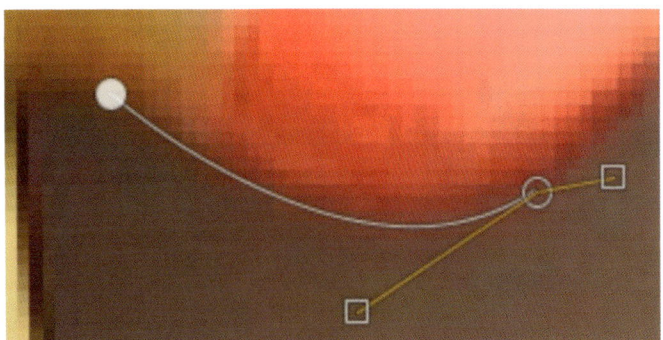

Then **Click & drag** the other handle to make the curve. When this looks good, we *click* the following node, *hold* the left mouse button down and *drag* it out a little bit again.

Click & drag the other handle to make the curve. Continue in this way until we are back at the first node.

Then we hover over it, *hold down* **Ctrl/Cmd** and, when the chain is visible, we *click* to close the path.

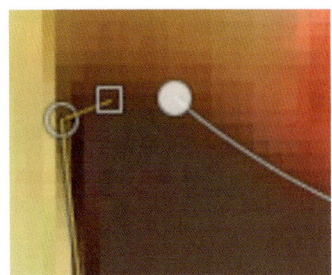

Press **Ctrl/Cmd + Shift + J** once more.

Now we can click the button **Selection from Path**, and there we have our selection.

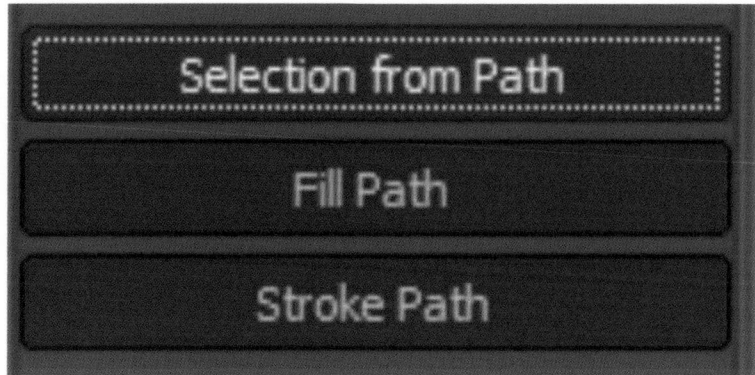

When we hit **B**, the path is invisible, but the **Paths Tool** is still active.

And there we have a simple and easy way, to make very accurate selections with the **Paths Tool**.

12. How to Save and Export Images

In this tutorial we're going to learn two ways how to save and export images in GIMP.

If you want to use the same image we'll be using, please download the image from our Facebook page.

Ready? There are two ways of saving images in Gimp.

The first way is to *save* it as an **.xcf** file.

To save your image as an **.xcf** file:

1. *Go* to **File**.

2. *Press* **Save** or **Save As.**

This goes via file, and then **Save** or **Save As**. **Xcf** is the file type specific to Gimp. There are almost no other programs that can open this file type. A big advantage of an **.xcf** file is, that it saves all information of the image, such as the quality, and it stores all the separate layers. The only thing an xcf file does not safe, are the undo actions of the previous work.

And we can not open an xcf file with other programs, as an actual image.

3. *Choose* where you want to *save* your image.

4. *Click* on **Save**.

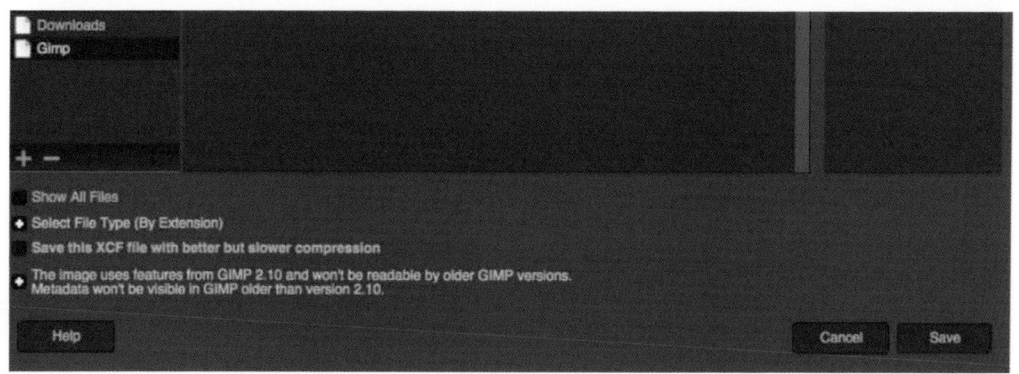

Show All Files

Select File Type (By Extension)

Save this XCF file with better but slower compression

The image uses features from GIMP 2.10 and won't be readable by older GIMP versions.
Metadata won't be visible in GIMP older than version 2.10.

Help   Cancel   Save

The second way is taking the file out of Gimp as an actual image.

To do this:

1. *Go* to **File**

2. *Select* **Export As.**

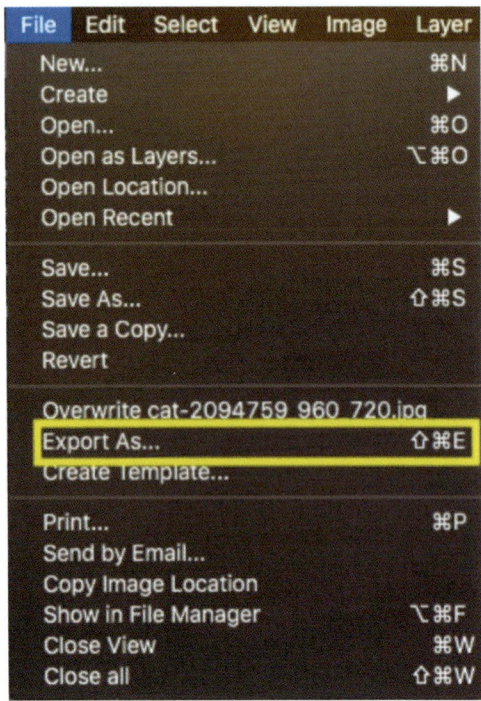

If we have already saved this particular image, we have the option to overwrite the source file. However, when we overwrite the image, we have lost all the information of the source file.

3. *Choose* where you want your image exported to.

Down here (see image), we can also *choose* a different **Extension**, like **jpeg**, **png**, **tiff**, **pdf**, and so on.

When we *click* on a certain extension, the extension of our image automatically changes.

When we already know what extension we want to use, we can also just type in the extension.

When we *save* or *export* an image, we usually see another window popping up (see image).

Here we can, if we are knowledgeable, *apply* **Advanced Options**.

The default values however are usually sufficient to give an excellent result.

The option **Save a Copy** (*click* on **File** and then on **Save a Copy**), can come in handy when we are working on a complex project and, for safety reasons, want to make an interim copy.

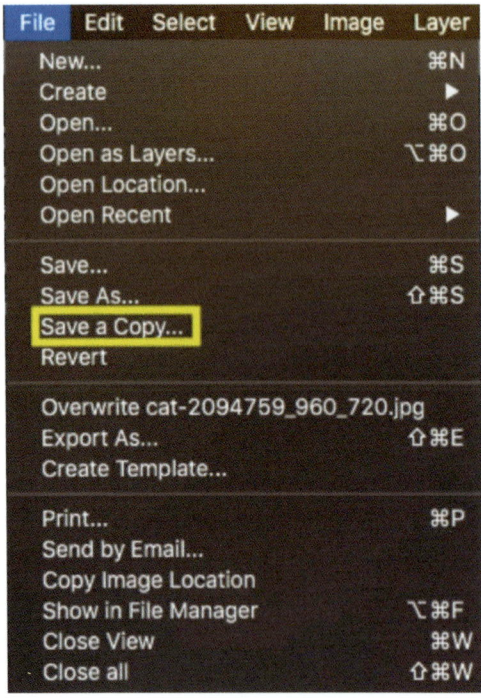

The source file as well as the current state of the image stay unaffected. This copy is an xcf file. Although Gimp is a quiet robust program, it still might be a good idea to make copies of your images before you start editing. So, if anything goes wrong, you still have your original files as a backup.

Now, you know **how to save and export images** in Gimp.

Thank you for purchasing this book.

Special Offer

Join our mailing list KuhlmanPublishing@yahoo.com and enjoy two free Learn GIMP tutorials totally free. We promise not to send you spam. Un-enroll anytime.

Printed in Great Britain
by Amazon

81567771R10047